THE
TOTALLY
STRAWBERRIES
COOKBOOK

D0724034

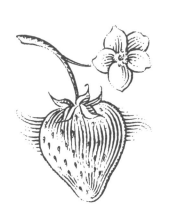

THE
TOTALLY
STRAWBERRIES
COOKBOOK

By Helene Siegel and Karen Gillingham

Illustrated by Carolyn Vibbert

CELESTIAL ARTS
BERKELEY, CALIFORNIA

Copyright © 1999 by Helene Siegel and Karen Gillingham.
Illustrations copyright © 1999 by Carolyn Vibbert.
All rights reserved. No part of this book may be reproduced or transmitted in any form or by any means, electronic or mechanical, including photocopying, recording, or by any information storage and retrieval system without permission in writing.

The Totally Strawberries Cookbook is produced by becker&mayer!, Ltd.
www.beckermayer.com

Printed in Singapore.

Cover design and illustration: Bob Greisen
Interior design and typesetting: Susan Hernday
Interior illustrations: Carolyn Vibbert

Library of Congress Cataloging-in-Publication Data
Siegel, Helene.
  The totally strawberries cookbook / by Helene Sigel and Karen Gillingham ; illustrated by Carolyn Vibbert.
      p.   cm.
    ISBN 0-89087-895-1
    1. Cookery (Strawberries)   I. Gillingham, Karen. II. Title.
TX813.S9S54   1999
641.6'475—dc21   98-33434
                                                                CIP

Celestial Arts Publishing
P.O. Box 7123
Berkeley, CA 94707

Look for all 28 *Totally* books at your local store!

FOR THOSE WHO KEEP GROWING
AND PICKING THE BERRIES

CONTENTS

INTRODUCTION

When I left New York to move to southern California I gave up the Manhattan skyline, New York taxis, and street-corner hot dogs. But I gained strawberries!

During my first season in California I remember being in a state of shock in early April. The mornings were still overcast and the temperature was hovering around sixty, but luscious-looking strawberries were everywhere. They were stacked in plastic baskets at the supermarket, street vendors were hawking them at traffic lights, and farmers markets had the crème de la crème. And they were selling them for a song! In New York, fresh strawberries were only sold in the best markets and were priced accordingly. Like small gems, they were to be savored only on rare occasions.

Here, the trick is to avoid taking our juicy little berries for granted. Like other Californians, for months on end I generously garnish my morning cereal with sliced strawberries, pack them whole in lunch boxes, and bake them into two favorite desserts—strawberry shortcake and elegant strawberry tarts. After the summer, things do slow down a bit. But strawberries are always out there. A decent, not-too-watery berry can always be found.

In case you need help getting your own strawberry season started, here are a few good ideas. Within you'll find pink drinks—alcoholic and non—bracing cold soups, a few delicate salads, spicy salsas, and plenty of fabulous desserts. But don't forget the standards.

Nothing is more elegant than perfect berries served simply and with style. Serve them piled high in beautiful bowls and baskets with a few choice accompaniments: whipped cream, white and brown sugar for sprinkling, balsamic vinegar, and even a glass of champagne. Cheers!

Curly locks, curly locks,
Wilt thou be mine?
Thou shalt not wash dishes
Nor yet feed the swine.
But sit on a cushion
And sew a fine seam,
And feed upon strawberries,
Sugar, and cream.
　　　　　—Nursery rhyme

SNACKS
AND
STARTERS

STRAWBERRY WATERMELON SOUP

This cool, bracing, very pink soup is best suited to a ladies' lunch or, served in mugs for sipping, or an outdoor barbecue.

4 cups rindless watermelon chunks, seeded
2 tablespoons sugar
1 pint strawberries, hulled
½ cup plain yogurt
juice of 1 lemon
ice cubes for serving (optional)
6 sprigs fresh mint for garnish

Place melon and sugar in food processor, and purée until smooth. Pour into mixing bowl.

Place berries in food processor and purée. Add yogurt and lemon juice and purée again. Pour into bowl with watermelon and stir well. Chill until ice cold.

Serve in chilled bowls (or with a few small ice cubes in the bottom of the bowl) with sprigs of mint as garnish.

SERVES 6

"We respond to strawberry fields or cherry orchards with a delight that a cabbage patch or even an elegant vegetable garden cannot provoke."

—Jane Grigson, Jane Grigson's Fruit Book

BERRY AND GOAT CHEESE SALAD

Who can resist goat cheese and greens—especially when highlighted by chunks of sweet berry?

8 thin slices baguette
$\frac{1}{4}$ cup softened goat cheese
8 cups mixed salad greens
1 cup strawberries, hulled and quartered
1 blood orange, peeled and sectioned
1 teaspoon honey
2 tablespoons sherry vinegar
$\frac{1}{4}$ cup heavy cream
salt and freshly ground pepper

Preheat oven to 450 degrees F. Place baguette slices on baking tray and toast in oven 5 minutes. Turn over and spread each with goat cheese. Return to oven and toast 5 minutes longer, to melt cheese. Set aside.

Combine the salad greens, berries, and orange sections in a large bowl. Toss well.

In a small bowl, whisk together honey, vinegar, cream, salt, and pepper to taste. Pour over the salad and toss well to coat evenly. Divide the salad into four portions and place on plates. Garnish each with two toasted baguette slices and serve.

SERVES 4

STRAWBERRY SPINACH SALAD

The delicacy of spinach goes well with fruit.

1 (6-ounce) bag clean spinach leaves
1 pint strawberries, hulled and halved
1 orange, peeled
balsamic vinegar
$\frac{1}{3}$ cup extra virgin olive oil
1 tablespoon chopped fresh basil *or*
    1 teaspoon dried
salt and pepper
$\frac{1}{4}$ cup toasted pine nuts

Place spinach in large salad bowl. Add berries. Holding orange over a glass measuring cup to collect juices, cut between the membranes to remove segments. Add orange segments to salad, leaving the juice in the cup.

Add enough vinegar to the juice in the cup to measure ½ cup. Gradually whisk in olive oil. Stir in basil and season to taste with salt and pepper. Pour dressing over salad and toss thoroughly. Scatter pine nuts over top.

SERVES 6

"You have to ask children and birds how cherries and strawberries taste."

  —Goethe

STRAWBERRY DUMPLINGS

These sweet fruit dumplings always remind Karen of her college days in the sixties.

5 to 6 cups strawberries, hulled and halved
3/4 cup sugar
1 cup all-purpose flour
1 1/2 teaspoons baking powder
1/4 teaspoon baking soda
1/4 teaspoon salt
1 cup heavy cream
additional sugar for sprinkling

Preheat oven to 400 degrees F.

In a shallow 2-quart casserole or baking dish, combine berries and sugar. Place in oven.

Meanwhile, mix flour, baking powder, soda, and salt in bowl. Stir in cream until smooth.

When strawberry mixture begins to bubble, about 8 minutes, remove from oven and drop dumpling dough by large spoonfuls over top, making about 8 dumplings. Sprinkle lightly with additional sugar. Return to oven and bake until dumplings are puffy and golden, about 10 minutes. Serve hot, or let cool slightly.

SERVES 4 TO 6

JAM AND CREAM CHEESE OMELET

Omelets with jam and cheese are handy to have in your weeknight repertoire of quick, easy, light meals.

1 teaspoon butter
2 eggs, lightly beaten
salt and freshly ground pepper
1 ounce cream cheese, softened and cut into
    small cubes
1 tablespoon "Strawberry Preserves" (see page 38)

Melt the butter in a small skillet over high heat. Season eggs with salt and pepper. Swirl eggs into pan and briefly cook until bottom is set. Reduce heat. Scatter cheese over eggs. Add jam to center. When eggs are set and cheese is melted, fold over, cook a few seconds longer, and serve.

SERVES 1

BREADS
AND
THINGS

STRAWBERRY CINNAMON MUFFINS

Store leftover muffins in the freezer in resealable bags. For a quick breakfast treat, simply reheat in the toaster oven at 350 degrees F for 10 minutes.

2 eggs
$2/3$ cup sugar
$1/2$ cup milk
$1/4$ cup plain yogurt
1 teaspoon vanilla
$1/2$ stick butter, melted and cooled
2 cups all-purpose flour
1 tablespoon baking powder
$1/4$ teaspoon salt
$1/4$ teaspoon cinnamon
$1 1/2$ cups firm strawberries, hulled and cut in chunks
"Pink Berry Glaze" (optional)

Preheat oven to 375 degrees F. Grease muffin tins or line with paper cups.

In a large mixing bowl, whisk together eggs and sugar until light. Add milk, yogurt, vanilla, and melted butter. Gently whisk.

In another bowl, combine flour, baking powder, salt, and cinnamon. Add to milk mixture and stir just until flour disappears. Gently stir in berries. Spoon thick batter into muffin cups to the top. Bake about 25 minutes, until tester comes out clean. Invert and cool on rack. For optional glaze, dip cooled muffin top into glaze. Return to rack to set.

MAKES 12

PINK BERRY GLAZE

- 2 large strawberries, hulled and halved
- 1 teaspoon lemon juice
- 1 cup confectioners' sugar

Place all of the ingredients in a blender and briefly process until smooth.

MAKES ENOUGH FOR 24 MUFFINS

LEMON BERRY TEA BREAD

Using preserves allows the bread to retain the bright red color of the berries and the intense flavor of the preserves.

1 stick butter, at room temperature
1 cup sugar
1 egg, lightly beaten
1½ cups all-purpose flour
½ teaspoon baking powder
½ teaspoon baking soda
½ teaspoon salt
½ teaspoon vanilla
2 teaspoons grated lemon zest
½ cup lemon juice
½ cup "Strawberry Preserves" (see page 38)

Preheat oven to 350 degrees F. Grease and flour 9 x 5 x 3-inch loaf pan.

In large mixing bowl, beat butter until smooth. Gradually add sugar, beating until light. Beat in egg.

Sift flour with baking powder, soda, and salt. Sprinkle about half of flour mixture over butter mixture, and gently beat until blended.

Combine vanilla, lemon zest, and juice. Add half of the liquid mixture to the butter mixture, and beat. Add remaining dry ingredients and liquid, and beat until well blended.

Pour into prepared pan. Drop strawberry preserves by large spoonfuls over top. Drag the blade of a table knife through preserves and batter to marbleize.

Bake about 45 minutes or until toothpick inserted in center comes out clean. Cool in pan on a rack 10 minutes, then turn out bread and cool completely.

MAKES 1 LOAF

EASY STRAWBERRY FOCACCIA

Cut this fruit-topped flat bread into small squares for nibbling with cocktails.

flour or cornmeal for dusting
1 (1-pound) loaf frozen white bread dough
2 tablespoons melted butter
1 quart strawberries, hulled, large ones cut in half
$\frac{1}{4}$ to $\frac{1}{2}$ cup sugar, preferably coarse

Preheat oven to 400 degrees F. Dust large baking sheet with flour or cornmeal.

Thaw bread dough according to package directions. Punch down dough and knead a few turns. Cut in half. Press each into a rough 8-inch round. Place on prepared baking sheet. Brush tops with butter. Pile berries in center of each round, leaving 1-inch border bare. Sprinkle berries with sugar to taste. Bake 5 to 7 minutes, or until puffed and golden. Cool and serve.

SERVES 6

STRAWBERRY TEA SANDWICHES

What could be more ladylike than thin, little, lighter-than-air strawberry sandwiches with afternoon tea?

16 thin slices raisin bread, preferably dark bread
1 (8-ounce) package cream cheese
1 pint strawberries, hulled and sliced lengthwise

Stack bread slices and trim off crusts, if desired. Spread each with a thin layer of cream cheese. Top half of the bread slices with a single layer of berry slices. Cover with remaining bread slices, making sandwiches. Cut into quarters, on the diagonal. Chill or serve.

SERVES 8

STRAWBERRY PANCAKES WITH MAPLE BERRY COMPOTE

These pancakes have a double dose of berries: once in the batter, and again in the syrup. Plain pancakes topped with sliced berries and whipped cream are also acceptable early-morning fare for berry fanatics.

1 cup all-purpose flour
1 teaspoon baking soda
1 tablespoon sugar
1/4 teaspoon salt
1 1/4 cups buttermilk
1 egg
2 tablespoons butter, melted
butter for coating griddle
2 cups sliced strawberries

Combine flour, baking soda, sugar, and salt in mixing bowl. Mix with fork.

In another bowl, whisk together the buttermilk, egg, and melted butter. Add the flour mixture to liquid, and stir just until combined.

Heat the skillet or griddle over medium-high heat. Lightly coat with butter. Drop batter, a quarter-cup at a time, on griddle, with plenty of space for spreading. Then press a few strawberry slices into each pancake. Fry until bubbles form and break on the pancake's surface and the bottom is browned. Flip and cook just until done, about 1 minute more. Serve with "Maple Berry Compote."

MAKES 12

MAPLE BERRY COMPOTE

$\frac{1}{2}$ cup maple syrup
1 cup sliced strawberries
2 teaspoons Grand Marnier (optional)

Combine all the ingredients in a serving pitcher. Let sit 1 hour at room temperature or chill up to 4 hours.

SERVES 4

GINGER CREAM SCONES WITH DRIED BERRIES

In case you were wondering what to do with those dried strawberries sold in health-food markets, here is a delicious gingered scone to serve with preserves, butter, and thickened cream.

2 cups all-purpose flour
⅓ cup sugar
1 tablespoon baking powder
½ teaspoon salt
½ cup dried strawberries
1 tablespoon candied ginger, finely chopped
1¼ cups heavy cream
cream and sugar for brushing

Preheat oven to 425 degrees F.

In large mixing bowl, combine flour, sugar, baking powder, and salt. Stir in berries and ginger. Add cream, stirring with fork until just moistened. Gather dough into ball, and transfer to floured surface.

Lightly knead and pat into 8-inch circle. Cut into eight wedges and place 1 inch apart on ungreased baking sheet. Brush tops with cream and sprinkle lightly with sugar. Bake until golden, about 12 minutes. Serve warm.

SERVES 8

The Word

Strawberry is derived from the Anglo-Saxon verb "to strew," or "spread." The name probably came from the strawberry plant's prolific production of runners that spread outward from the central plant. From "strew" came the earlier name "streabergan," which eventually became "straberry," "streberie," "straibery," "strauberry," and finally "strawberry."

How to Choose and Store Berries

The best-tasting strawberries can be found at farmers markets and farm stands between the months of April and June. Since they do not ripen off the vine, look for firm, red, smooth berries without white patches. If purchasing at the supermarket, turn over the basket and reject those with bruised or moldy berries. (If you must purchase bruised fruit, trim off and discard mold immediately to prevent its spread.)

At home, store strawberries in the refrigerator in the original basket, with a paper towel beneath to absorb moisture. Small market baskets measure 1 pint, and large ones, 1 quart. Clean berries only when ready to serve or cook. Lightly rinse under cold water and shake off excess moisture. Remove stems after washing. Once rinsed, berries will spoil quickly. Ripe berries keep in the refrigerator as long as four days.

SPREADS,
SALSAS,
AND
SAUCES

BERRY MANGO SALSA

With its pretty colors and spicy punch, this sprightly salsa is perfect for cutting the richness of a flourless chocolate cake or chocolate terrine. It's also fantastic as a topping for ice cream or sorbet, or sprinkled over slices of French toast for an elegant brunch.

1 cup pineapple, finely diced
½ cup mango, finely diced
1 cup strawberries, hulled and finely diced
1 tablespoon crystallized ginger, minced
2 tablespoons lemon juice
2 teaspoons brown sugar

Combine all of the ingredients in a bowl and mix well. Store in the refrigerator up to 2 days.

MAKES 2 CUPS, SERVES 8

STRAWBERRY COULIS

Here is the quickest way to make strawberry sauce for dressing up dessert plates.

1 pint strawberries, hulled
3 tablespoons confectioners' sugar
1 teaspoon lemon juice

Combine all of the ingredients in a food processor or blender and purée until smooth. Store in the refrigerator.

MAKES ABOUT 1 CUP

The Fruit
The North American strawberry is an herbaceous peren-nial that produces vines close to the ground. Technically, the little specks on the berry's skin are not seeds at all. In fact, each whole strawberry is a seed that grows from the stalk's fleshy tip and enlarges into a fleshy receptacle called a strawberry.

STRAWBERRY BUTTER

Serve as a low-fat substitute for butter when calorie-counting takes priority.

- ½ pound strawberries, hulled
- ¼ cup strawberry juice or nectar, *or* apple cider
- 2 tablespoons honey
- ¼ teaspoon vanilla
- pinch of cinnamon

Combine all the ingredients in a medium saucepan. Bring to a boil, reduce to a simmer, and cook until berries are soft. Drain, reserving the juices.

Place the berries in a food processor or blender and purée until smooth. Pass through a fine strainer. If too thick, add a few drops of reserved juices to thin to taste.

MAKES ½ CUP

FRESH STRAWBERRY-CREAM CHEESE SPREAD

Strawberry spread is a nice treat to serve with toasted bagels for a summer brunch.

1 cup chopped, stemmed strawberries
1 tablespoon sugar
1 (8-ounce) package cream cheese, softened
2 tablespoons heavy cream
1 teaspoon vanilla

Combine the berries and sugar in a small bowl and let sit 5 minutes.

With electric mixer, whip the cream cheese, heavy cream, and vanilla until light and fluffy. Add sweetened berries and gently mix just to combine. Keeps in the refrigerator 2 days.

SERVES 6

STRAWBERRY PRESERVES

This is the best excuse for purchasing a flat of beautiful berries at the farm stand—classic and pure strawberry preserves.

> 2 quarts strawberries, hulled and lightly crushed
> ¼ cup lemon juice
> 7 cups sugar

Combine berries, lemon juice, and sugar in a large pot. Bring to a boil over medium heat, stirring occasionally, until sugar dissolves. Reduce heat and cook, stirring frequently, until thermometer registers 221 to 224 degrees F, or until thickened to taste, about 30 minutes. Remove from heat, and skim off foam. Ladle into hot sterilized jars, leaving ¼-inch headspace. Seal with lids. Place jars in large pan with water to cover. Boil for 10 minutes. Cool and store in a cool place.

MAKES 8 CUPS

STRAWBERRY TOPPING
FOR SUNDAES

This is a very easy sauce to make. Keep it on hand in the fridge for quick strawberry sundaes.

- ¹/₂ cup red currant jelly
- 2 tablespoons cassis
- 1 pint strawberries, hulled and quartered

Combine the jelly and cassis in a medium saucepan. Bring to a boil over medium heat, stirring occasionally, until smooth, about 2 minutes. Add berries, reduce heat to medium-low, and cook until berries are soft, about 5 minutes. Remove from heat and mash with a fork until pieces are small. Cool and refrigerate as long as 2 weeks. Serve cold over ice cream—hot fudge sauce is optional.

SERVES 4

California Strawberries

California produces 80 percent of the nation's strawberries on about 23,000 acres of land. Berries are harvested every month but December. They are picked, sorted, packed by hand and rushed to shipping facilities. Then, within 24 hours, they are shipped on refrigerated trucks all over the country. Since strawberries grow best in areas of warm, sunny days and foggy nights, the coastline is perfect. Farming centers are Oxnard (which hosts an annual strawberry festival), San Diego, Orange County, Santa Maria, and the Salinas-Watsonville area. The two most popular varieties are the slightly acidic Seascape and the sweeter Chandler.

BAKING
WITH
BERRIES

STRAWBERRY TART

We love the simple elegance of this French-style tart.

1¼ cups cake flour
½ cup confectioners' sugar
pinch of salt
6 tablespoons butter, cold, cut in pieces
1 egg yolk beaten with ½ teaspoon vanilla
1 cup strawberry jam
1 tablespoon lemon juice
1 quart large strawberries, hulled
whipped cream *or* vanilla ice cream
    for serving

To make the crust, in a food processor fitted with the metal blade, combine flour, sugar, and salt. Pulse to mix. Add butter and pulse to break into small pieces. Add yolk mixture. Pulse until mixture is crumbly and holds together when pressed. Transfer to a sheet of plastic wrap, press into disk shape, wrap, and chill 1 hour.

On a lightly floured board, roll out dough and line a 9-inch round tart pan. Cover with foil, prick all over with a fork, and chill ½ hour.

Preheat oven to 350 degrees F.

Fill foil-lined tart pan with weights (rice or beans) and bake 15 minutes. Then remove foil and weights, place back in the oven, and bake 20 to 25 minutes longer, until golden. Cool in pan on rack.

To make filling, place jam and lemon juice in a small pan, and cook over medium heat, stirring occasionally, until melted and smooth. Cool slightly. Brush the tart's bottom crust all over with warm jam. Then, piercing each berry at the top with a fork, dip one at a time into hot jam to coat. Arrange berries, trimmed-side down, in a single layer in tart shell. Chill until serving time. Serve with whipped cream or ice cream, if desired.

MAKES 1 TART

STRAWBERRIES AND CREAM LAYER CAKE

Feel free to substitute your favorite from-scratch sponge cake for this classic combination. After tasting a slice, Helene's six-year-old son requested this cake for his next birthday.

1 package yellow cake mix
1 pint *plus* 5 small strawberries
2 tablespoons granulated sugar
1½ cups heavy cream, cold
¼ cup confectioners' sugar
2 tablespoons sour cream *or* mascarpone
1 teaspoon vanilla

Butter and flour two 8-inch round cake pans. Prepare cake mix according to directions. Cool in pans on rack ½ hour. Invert to remove, and cool.

Meanwhile, hull all of the berries except the five small ones. (Reserve these for decoration.) Slice half the berries and place in a bowl. Add granulated sugar and toss. Let sit 1 hour to soften, then lightly mash with a fork so slices remain. Cut the remaining berries in half lengthwise, and reserve.

Whip the cream with a whisk until it begins to thicken. Add confectioners' sugar, sour cream, and vanilla, and continue whisking until soft peaks form. Refrigerate until ready to assemble cake.

To assemble: Place one cake layer upside down on a platter. Spoon on the sliced berries and their juices in an even layer. Top with a thin layer of cream. Place the second layer, right-side up, over cream. Cover top and sides with remaining cream. Decorate top with halved berries, starting from outer edge and working toward the center. Fill center with five unhulled berries. Store in the refrigerator.

SERVES 8

STRAWBERRY LEMON CHEESECAKE

Lemon brings this smooth, rich cheesecake into balance.

2 cups graham crackers, finely ground
6 tablespoons butter, melted
2 pounds cream cheese
1 cup plus 2 tablespoons sugar
3 eggs
2 teaspoons lemon oil *or* 1 tablespoon grated lemon zest
1½ teaspoons vanilla
¼ cup currant jelly
2 tablespoons water
2½ pints strawberries, hulled

Preheat oven to 325 degrees F.

With a spoon, mix together the cracker crumbs and butter. Press into bottom and ½ inch up sides of a 10-inch springform pan. Bake 5 minutes and remove.

In large bowl of electric mixer, beat cheese at low speed until smooth. Beat in 1 cup of sugar. Add eggs one at a time, and beat until smooth. Beat in lemon oil or zest and vanilla until light and fluffy. Pour into crust in pan, and bake until center is set, about 1 hour. Cool on rack 1 hour. Then transfer to refrigerator and chill 4 hours.

Make a glaze by combining currant jelly, water, and remaining 2 tablespoons of sugar in small pot. Bring to a boil, and simmer 3 minutes, skimming top. Cool slightly.

Remove sides of cake pan and place on serving platter. Arrange berries in an even layer, cut-side down, over top of cake. Dab top of berries with glaze and chill 3 hours longer. Store in the refrigerator.

SERVES 8

STRAWBERRY PIE

Here is a traditional single-crust strawberry pie. Gussy it up with a bottom layer of custard or whipped cream if you wish, though it is not necessary.

GLAZE

1 pint strawberries, hulled and chopped
½ cup sugar
2 tablespoons cornstarch
2 tablespoons water

PIE

1 prebaked 9-inch pie shell
1 quart strawberries, hulled
1 cup heavy cream, whipped
3 tablespoons confectioners' sugar

To make glaze, purée the berries in a food processor or blender. Combine with sugar in a small pot. Bring to a boil. Meanwhile, in a small bowl, stir together the cornstarch and water until a smooth paste forms. Pour the cornstarch mixture into the boiling berry purée. Cook, whisking constantly, until smooth and thick, about 1 minute. Cool slightly.

Spread about ½ cup glaze in bottom of pie shell. Arrange the berries in a single layer, cut-side down, over glaze. Spoon remaining glaze over berries and chill. Before serving, whisk the cream with sugar until peaks form. Decorate pie with cream or serve alongside.

MAKES 1 PIE

"Strawberries, and only strawberries, could now be thought of or spoken of."
      —*Jane Austen,* Emma

STRAWBERRY THUMBPRINT COOKIES

This classic American cookie holds the bright berry jam in a little crater in the center, for quick licks.

1½ cups almonds, finely ground, with skins
1½ cups all-purpose flour
½ teaspoon baking soda
½ teaspoon salt
1 stick butter, softened
½ cup brown sugar
2 eggs, separated
2 teaspoons amaretto *or* ½ teaspoon almond extract
¼ cup strawberry jam

Preheat oven to 350 degrees F. Lightly grease cookie sheets. Place ³/₄ cup ground almonds in a small bowl and set aside.

Toss together ³/₄ cup ground almonds, flour, baking soda, and salt.

In another large bowl, cream butter until light and smooth. Add sugar and beat until fluffy. Beat in egg yolks and amaretto or extract. Add flour mixture and gently beat until flour disappears and dough holds a shape when pressed.

In a small bowl, whisk egg whites until foamy. Break off tablespoon-size pieces of dough and roll between palms to form a ball. Dip each in egg whites to coat, then roll in reserved almonds. Place on cookie sheet, and press crater into center with the back of a ¹/₂-teaspoon measure or your thumb tip.

Bake about 15 minutes, until nuts on edges just begin to color. While still hot, immediately re-press hole in center. Transfer to racks to cool slightly, then fill each with ¹/₂ teaspoon jam.

MAKES ABOUT 20

STRAWBERRY SHORTCAKES

All the parts can be prepared in advance and assembled at serving time in this all-American favorite. Combine with mixed berries or remain a strawberry purist, as you wish.

1½ pints strawberries, hulled and sliced
1½ tablespoons sugar
1 cup heavy cream, cold
3 tablespoons confectioners' sugar
2 teaspoons vanilla *or* Grand Marnier
8 "Rosemary Cream Biscuits" (see page 54)

Combine strawberries and sugar in a bowl and let sit at least 1 hour at room temperature or up to 7 hours in the refrigerator. A syrup will form in the bottom of the bowl.

Pour cream into chilled mixing bowl and whisk with balloon whisk at low speed, until cream starts to thicken. Turn speed to high, drizzle in sugar and vanilla or liqueur, and whisk until soft peaks form. Whipped cream may be kept in the refrigerator for 1 day.

To serve: Slice each biscuit in half and place the bottoms on serving plates. Top each with a generous spoonful of strawberries, and spoon the syrup evenly over all. Spoon the whipped cream over the berries to taste and then cover with the top piece of biscuit. (Berries and cream spilling out of the biscuit is desirable.) Serve immediately.

MAKES 8

"A bite of real strawberry shortcake...is a mouthful of contrast. The rich, sweet cream, the tart juicy berries, and the sour crumbly texture of biscuit all refuse to amalgam into a single flavor..."
—John Thorne, Simple Cooking

ROSEMARY CREAM BISCUITS

2 cups all-purpose flour
1 tablespoon baking powder
1 tablespoon sugar
½ teaspoon salt
¼ teaspoon minced rosemary leaves
1¼ cups heavy cream
4 tablespoons butter, melted
cinnamon sugar for sprinkling (optional but
    delicious for shortcakes)

Preheat oven to 425 degrees F.

Combine flour, baking powder, sugar, salt, and rosemary in a large mixing bowl. Mix with a fork. Gradually pour in about 1 cup of the cream, stirring constantly with a wooden spoon to moisten evenly. Drizzle in remaining cream, turning dough by hand until just moist enough to hold together.

Turn out onto a floured board and knead about 1 minute. Pat dough into circle, and then lightly roll to about ½-inch thickness.

Cut out with 3-inch round fluted cutter or glass dipped in flour. Gather dough scraps, and reroll, being careful to handle lightly. Transfer to uncoated baking sheet, brush tops with butter, and sprinkle with cinnamon sugar, if desired. Bake about 15 minutes, until edges are lightly browned. Cool on racks.

MAKES 10

"Put them on the table in a glass dish, piling them high and lightly, send around powdered sugar with them and cream, that the guests may help themselves. It is not economical perhaps, but it is a healthful and pleasant style of serving them...."
　　　—Marion Harland, 1883

STRAWBERRY RHUBARB COBBLER

Cobblers, biscuit-topped fruit desserts, are best served warm from the oven and topped with some chilled cream or vanilla ice cream.

1 pound rhubarb, sliced in ½-inch lengths (about 3 cups)
1½ pints strawberries, hulled and halved
½ cup sugar
2 tablespoons cornstarch
1 recipe "Rosemary Cream Biscuits" dough (see page 54), rosemary omitted
melted butter
sugar for sprinkling

Preheat oven to 375 degrees F. Lightly butter a shallow 2-quart ovenproof casserole.

Drop the rhubarb in rapidly boiling salted water and cook less than 1 minute. Drain and dry.

In a mixing bowl, combine rhubarb, berries, sugar, and cornstarch. Stir well and let sit while preparing the biscuit dough.

Transfer fruit mixture to casserole. Cut out dough in 2-inch rounds and arrange in single layer over fruit. Brush biscuit tops with butter, sprinkle with sugar, and bake until top is brown and puffy, about ½ hour. Serve warm.

SERVES 8

"Toujours strawberries and cream."
—Samuel Johnson

STRAWBERRY PAVLOVA

*Pavlova is a meringuelike cake from the classic
French repertoire. It can be made several days
ahead and stored in an airtight container at room
temperature.*

4 egg whites, at room temperature
1/4 teaspoon salt
1/8 teaspoon cream of tartar
1/2 cup sugar
2 teaspoons vanilla
1 teaspoon vinegar
1 tablespoon cold water
1 tablespoon cornstarch
1/2 cup superfine sugar
1 cup heavy cream, whipped
1 pint strawberries, hulled, halved, and
    sweetened to taste
mint leaves for garnish

Preheat oven to 300 degrees F. Line a baking sheet with waxed or parchment paper. Lightly grease paper.

In large bowl of an electric mixer, whisk egg whites with salt and cream of tartar until soft peaks form. Whisk in ½ cup sugar, 1 tablespoon at a time. Add vanilla, vinegar, water, and cornstarch, and continue beating until stiff peaks form. Add superfine sugar all at once, and beat just until incorporated.

Turn out mixture in mound on prepared baking sheet. Using a wide spatula, shape into 8-inch round. Bake 10 minutes without opening the oven door. Reduce oven temperature to 200 degrees F and bake 20 minutes longer. Turn off oven. After 30 minutes, remove from oven and cool to room temperature. (The center will fall.)

To serve, transfer cake to a serving platter. Mound whipped cream in center of cake. Arrange sliced berries in concentric circles over cream. Garnish with mint.

SERVES 8 TO 10

STRAWBERRY ROLY-POLY CHOCOLATE CAKE

Chocolate and strawberries rolled together in a cake—yum!

vegetable oil for coating
1/3 cup cake flour
1/4 cup unsweetened cocoa powder
3/4 teaspoon baking soda
1/4 teaspoon salt
4 eggs, room temperature, separated
1/2 cup sugar
1/4 cup "Strawberry Preserves" (see page 38)
1 1/2 cups strawberries, hulled and sliced
1 cup heavy cream, whipped
whole strawberries for garnish

Preheat oven to 400 degrees F. Line a 15 x 10-inch jelly-roll pan with waxed or parchment paper. Lightly coat paper with oil.

Sift flour with cocoa, soda, and salt into a medium bowl.

In another medium bowl, beat egg yolks with ¼ cup of the sugar until light, about 3 minutes.

In another clean mixer bowl, whisk whites until frothy. Gradually add 2 tablespoons sugar and whisk until firm, about 1 minute longer. Stir one-third of whites into yolk mixture, then carefully fold in remaining whites. Fold in dry ingredients, one-third at a time. Spread batter in prepared pan, and bake until center springs back when pressed, about 12 minutes. Cool 10 minutes.

Sprinkle remaining 2 tablespoons sugar evenly over 19-inch-long sheet of waxed paper. Turn out cake onto waxed paper and peel away paper lining. Starting at one long side, roll up cake in waxed paper. Twist ends of paper to secure, and chill at least 3 hours.

To fill cake, remove from refrigerator and unroll on a work counter, resting cake on the paper. Spread preserves evenly over cake. Sprinkle sliced strawberries evenly over preserves, leaving 1-inch border along edge. Spread about two-thirds of whipped cream over berries. Roll cake to enclose filling, and wrap in waxed paper. Place on a tray, seam-side down, and chill at least 1 hour longer.

To serve, unwrap and place on a serving tray. Frost with remaining whipped cream and garnish with berries. Cut in slices to serve.

SERVES 8

RICH
DESSERTS

STRAWBERRY CREAM COCKTAIL

Serve this elegant dessert in a glass dish or martini glass. Top with the "Berry Mango Salsa" (see page 34) for added color and spice.

1 (15-ounce) container ricotta cheese
½ cup mascarpone *or* sour cream
¼ cup confectioners' sugar
½ cup cassis
1 pint strawberries, hulled and sliced
½ cup blackberries

With an electric mixer, beat together ricotta, mascarpone or sour cream, and confectioners' sugar until smooth and light.

Spoon 2 tablespoons of cassis into the bottom of four dessert dishes or wineglasses. Top each with a portion of sweetened cheese. Cover with plastic and chill until serving time. Before serving, mix together the sliced strawberries and blackberries. Spoon over the cheese in each dish and serve.

SERVES 4

European Berries

Strawberries have been cultivated in Europe since the Renaissance. In 1368, King Charles V of France had 1200 strawberry plants planted in the royal gardens of the Louvre, setting the stage for their acceptance by the masses. By the mid-fifteenth century, the street sellers of Paris were selling them everywhere. And they remain a prized ingredient today. It is the rare pastry shop that doesn't display a brilliant red strawberry tart in its window. Strawberries are eaten on honeymoon mornings to increase amour by the French. And in Norse legend, the goddess of marriage is Goddess Friga, or "strawberry." As for the English, what could be more correct than a cool, silver bowl of strawberries and cream? Throughout Europe, tiny flavor-concentrated varieties such as fraises des bois *in France and* fragioloni *in Italy can be found at summer markets.*

FRESH STRAWBERRY ICE CREAM

Nothing sold in a box could ever taste as fresh as this—a real treat for the beginning of the harvest in April.

2½ cups half-and-half
4 egg yolks
½ cup plus 2 tablespoons sugar
¼ teaspoon vanilla
1 pint strawberries, hulled and quartered

Pour the half-and-half into a heavy saucepan and bring to a boil. Remove from heat.

In a bowl, beat the egg yolks and ½ cup sugar until pale and smooth. Stir one-quarter of the hot half-and-half into the egg mixture. Then pour the yolk mixture into the warm pan. Cook over low heat, stirring constantly, until thick enough to coat a spoon, about 3 minutes. Stir in vanilla. Cool to room temperature, cover with plastic, and refrigerate at least 4 hours.

An hour before making the ice cream, in a bowl, combine the berries with 2 tablespoons of sugar and let sit 1 hour. Then mash the berries with a fork until they are bite-size. Stir into the chilled custard mixture and pour into the ice cream maker. Follow the manufacturer's directions. Transfer to a container and freeze 2 hours before serving.

SERVES 6

"This is the wonder of all the fruits growing naturally in these parts...I have many times seen as many as would fill a good ship...The Indians bruise them in a mortar, and mix them with meal and make strawberry bread."

—*Roger Williams of Rhode Island, 1643*

STRAWBERRY CRÈME BRÛLÉE

For true custard lovers, here is a mixture that doesn't stint on richness.

4 cups heavy cream
10 egg yolks
1½ cups sugar
¾ teaspoon vanilla
1 pint strawberries, hulled and sliced

For such a sensuous fruit, strawberries are exceedingly virtuous. They are fat- and cholesterol-free, contain only sixty calories a cup, and are high in vitamin C, folic acid, potassium, and fiber. And they taste delicious!

Pour the cream into a heavy saucepan and bring to a boil. Remove from heat.

In a bowl, beat the egg yolks and 1 cup of sugar until pale and smooth. Stir 1 cup of the hot cream into the egg mixture. Then pour the yolk mixture into the cream in the pan. Cook over low heat, stirring constantly, until thick enough to coat a spoon, about 3 minutes. Stir in vanilla.

Divide the berries into eight portions and place in eight ovenproof dessert bowls. Pour the custard mixture over all. Cool to room temperature, then cover and chill 4 hours to 2 days.

Before serving, preheat the broiler. Place the custard dishes on a baking tray, sprinkle each with the remaining sugar, and place under (but not too close to) the broiler. Broil just until tops are browned and set. Remove and serve.

SERVES 8

STRAWBERRY MOUSSE

This pale pink mousse will keep in the refrigerator for as long as 4 hours.

2 (¼-ounce) envelopes unflavored gelatin
⅓ cup water
1 quart strawberries, hulled and halved
½ cup sugar
¼ cup strawberry liqueur
1 tablespoon lemon juice
¾ cup heavy cream, cold
whole strawberries for garnish

Sprinkle gelatin over water and set aside until softened, about 5 minutes.

Purée berries with sugar in blender or food processor. Transfer to a large bowl.

Place bowl of softened gelatin in a pan with enough water to rise halfway up the sides of the bowl. Set over medium heat until gelatin is completely dissolved, or microwave on medium-high about 30 seconds.

Whisk dissolved gelatin, liqueur, and lemon juice into puréed berry mixture until thoroughly blended. Chill until it is consistency of egg whites.

Whip cream until thick but not stiff. Fold one-third of the cream into berry mixture to lighten. Fold in remaining cream. Chill until set, about 1 hour. Whisk just to lighten. Spoon mixture into individual dessert dishes and chill until serving time. Garnish with whole berries to serve.

SERVES 6

STRAWBERRY NAPOLEONS

Yogurt replaces cream in this lightweight version of the French classic. Look for frozen puff pastry in the supermarket freezer, next to frozen cakes.

1 quart plain yogurt
$3/4$ cup brown sugar
1 teaspoon vanilla
flour for dusting
$1/2$ ($17^1/4$-ounce) package frozen puff pastry sheets, thawed
$1/4$ cup "Strawberry Preserves" (see page 38), warmed in microwave 30 seconds
3 cups strawberries, hulled and sliced
$1/2$ cup confectioners' sugar
2 teaspoons water *or* milk

A day in advance, place yogurt in colander lined with cheesecloth. Set colander in bowl and cover with plastic wrap. Refrigerate at least 12 hours. Empty drained yogurt into bowl, and whisk in brown sugar and vanilla. Set aside.

Preheat oven to 400 degrees F. Dust baking tray with flour.

Unfold pastry sheet and cut along fold lines to make three rectangles. Arrange at least 1 inch apart on prepared baking sheet and bake until golden and crisp, about 15 minutes. Cool on wire rack.

Carefully split each rectangle in half lengthwise. Set aside two top rectangles. Spread preserves over cut sides of four remaining rectangles, then scatter berries over preserves. Stir yogurt to blend any undissolved sugar. Spoon over berries. Set one rectangle on top of another, then cover with a reserved rectangle. Repeat with remaining rectangles.

In small bowl, combine confectioners' sugar and water or milk. Mix well, adding more liquid if needed, to make a thin glaze. Drizzle over pastries. Carefully slice into six smaller rectangles each. Store in the refrigerator.

MAKES 12

The Great American Strawberry

The native American strawberry, Fragaria virginiana, *also known as Little Scarlet, was found growing abundantly by the first settlers. As a colonist recorded in his journal, "wee can not sett downe foote but tred on strawberries." Native Americans called them heart-seed berries and ground them with corn-meal to make strawberry bread, while Europeans just gathered strawberries and ate them out of hand. That sublime dessert strawberry shortcake was an American creation. Strawberries were not cultivated commercially until the mid-1800s and spread with the expansion of refrigerated railcars.*

LIGHT
ENDINGS

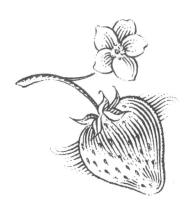

CELESTIAL SUMMER SOUP

Serve this elegant cold dessert on a sweltering summer night by candlelight. Your guests will never forget it.

½ cup sugar
½ cup water
1 pint strawberries, hulled and chopped
2 tablespoons cassis
1½ cups cold champagne
1 pint berry sorbet such as blackberry, raspberry, *or* marionberry
mint sprigs for garnish

In advance, combine the sugar and water in a pan. Bring to a boil and simmer, stirring occasionally, until clear.

Purée the strawberries with cassis in a blender or food processor. Stir together the purée and sugar syrup. Place in a container and chill at least 4 hours.

To serve, open the champagne and stir into cold berry purée. Let the fizzing subside. Arrange a scoop of sorbet in each of four soup bowls. Pour in the cold champagne mixture. Garnish with mint, and serve.

SERVES 4

CHOCOLATE-DIPPED STRAWBERRIES

Adding shortening to the chocolate makes it more pliable. If you prefer your chocolate coatings more brittle, simply omit the shortening. Chilling is also optional, but if you prefer a contrast of flavors and textures, serve the berries cold.

10 large strawberries, with stems for dipping
4 ounces bittersweet chocolate, chopped
2 teaspoons vegetable shortening (optional)

Wash the berries and pat dry. Have ready a tray lined with foil or parchment paper.

In the top of a double boiler or a bowl nested in a pot of shallow boiling water, melt the chocolate with vegetable shortening (if desired) until smooth. Dip the berries in the chocolate one at a time, holding them by the stem. Place on their sides on tray, until chocolate is set. Keep in the refrigerator as long as a day.

VARIATIONS:
For milk or white chocolate-dipped berries, omit the shortening. Other good fruits for dipping are halved orange slices and bananas thickly sliced on the diagonal.

In Napoleonic France, the extravagant Madame Tallien regularly added twenty-two pounds of crushed strawberries to her bath to maintain her soft and satiny skin.

STRAWBERRY GRANITA

Granitas are easy-to-make, slushy Italian ices.

1 cup sugar
½ cup water
1 quart strawberries, hulled and halved
¼ cup orange liqueur such as Cointreau *or*
    Grand Marnier
1 tablespoon lemon juice
whole strawberries and mint sprigs for garnish

Combine sugar and water in saucepan. Bring to a boil. Reduce heat to medium-high and cook, stirring frequently, about 3 minutes, or until sugar is dissolved. Let cool.

Combine berries, liqueur, lemon juice, and cooled sugar syrup in blender. Process until puréed. Strain, if desired. Pour purée into ice cube trays or 9-inch-square cake pan, and freeze.

Remove from freezer 10 minutes before serving. Turn out frozen cubes into food processor and pulse just until granular. Or break up mixture in a pan, turn out into a bowl and break up with a fork. Serve immediately, garnished with whole berries and mint.

SERVES 4 TO 6

STRAWBERRY SORBET WITH MELON

Here is another elegant presentation for sorbet in the summertime. Serve it over thinly sliced, ice-cold melon.

1 cup sugar
²/₃ cup water
2 tablespoons light corn syrup
1 quart strawberries, hulled and halved
1 chilled cantaloupe *or* honeydew melon, sliced into thin wedges and peeled

Combine sugar, water, and corn syrup in a saucepan and stir over low heat until sugar is dissolved. Raise heat and bring to a boil until clear. Remove from heat and set aside to cool slightly.

Place berries in food processor, and purée. Strain into a large bowl, pressing with the back of a large spoon to extract as much juice as possible. Add cooled syrup, and stir to blend. Chill 1 hour.

Transfer mixture to ice cream maker, and prepare according to manufacturer's directions. (Or pour into 8-inch-square pan, cover, and freeze until solid. Remove from freezer, and break into chunks. Place in processor and pulse until smooth.) Transfer mixture to freezer container and freeze until firm, at least 4 hours. Remove from freezer 15 minutes before serving.

Arrange several melon slices on six dessert plates. Arrange scoops of sorbet over melon and serve.

SERVES 6

STRAWBERRIES WITH BALSAMIC VINEGAR

We like to encourage guests to eat with their fingers. It helps everyone relax.

strawberries, with stems
sugar
balsamic vinegar

Wash and dry the berries and place on a platter or serving bowl.

Arrange a dessert plate for each guest with a mixture of a tablespoon of sugar and 2 teaspoons balsamic vinegar on it. To serve, pass berries in the bowl. Hold berries by stems and dip in mixture.

COLD PEACH AND STRAWBERRY COMPOTE

Use sweet, ripe peaches to make the most of this flavorful, easy dessert.

2 pints strawberries, hulled
3 ripe peaches, pitted and sliced
2 tablespoons sugar
2 tablespoons orange liqueur, such
    as Grand Marnier
¼ cup orange juice

Cut half of the strawberries into quarters. Combine in a mixing bowl with peaches.

Roughly chop the remaining strawberries and place in a food processor or blender. Add sugar, Grand Marnier, and orange juice. Purée until smooth and pour over the fruit in the bowl. Stir and toss to combine. Cover and chill 6 hours to 2 days. Serve cold in dessert bowls.

SERVES 6

STRAWBERRY ICE CREAM SANDWICHES

Here is a great interactive food for a child's ice cream party.

- strawberry ice cream
- vanilla-flavored wafers *or* oatmeal cookies
- sprinkles for decoration (optional)

Remove ice cream from freezer, and soften 10 to 15 minutes.

Place about 1½ tablespoons of ice cream on the bottom of a cookie. With a small spatula or back of a spoon, flatten slightly. Top with another cookie, and press to flatten into a sandwich. Run the back of the spoon along the edges to push back any oozing ice cream. If desired, roll edges in a bowl of sprinkles to coat. Transfer to a plate, and freeze until ice cream sets again. Then store in individual plastic baggies in freezer.

DRINKS
IN THE
PINK

STRAWBERRY ICE BLENDED

This light-pink, frothy drink is as healthful as it is pretty.

2 cups ice cubes
1 ripe banana, peeled and cut in chunks
10 large strawberries, hulled and halved
1½ cups low-fat milk
3 tablespoons honey

Place the ice in a blender and crush. Add remaining ingredients, and purée until light and frothy, about ½ minute. Serve cold.

MAKES 5 CUPS

MANGO STRAWBERRY SMOOTHIE

Acidic berries and limes create a good counterpoint to the rich flavor and texture of mango.

1 cup ice cubes
1 ripe mango, peeled, pitted, and cubed
8 large *or* 16 medium strawberries, hulled and halved
½ cup plain yogurt
½ cup orange juice
2 tablespoons honey
2 tablespoons lime juice

Place the ice in a blender and crush. Add remaining ingredients and briefly process until frothy. Serve cold over ice.

MAKES 4 CUPS

STRAWBERRY MILK SHAKE

Nothing is easier to make or more satisfying for the seriously strawberry-obsessed.

2½ scoops softened strawberry ice cream
½ cup milk
2 large *or* 4 small strawberries, hulled and
    chopped

In a blender, combine all of the ingredients. Process on high until smooth and frothy. Serve cold.

MAKES 1 CUP

STRAWBERRY LEMONADE

This is a favorite of ours from the strawberry festival held each spring in Oxnard, one of the berry-growing centers in southern California.

1 quart strawberries, hulled and halved
1 cup lemon juice
4 cups sugar
cold water
lemon slices and whole strawberries for garnish

To make syrup, place berries in a nonreactive pan with lemon juice and sugar. Bring to a boil, and cook, stirring, until sugar dissolves. Let cool. Strain, pressing with the back of a large spoon to extract juice. Strain again, then transfer to refrigerator and chill.

To make lemonade, mix 1 part strawberry syrup with 3 parts water and pour over ice in glass. Garnish with lemon slices and whole berries.

MAKES ABOUT 3 CUPS SYRUP, ENOUGH FOR 10 GLASSES

STRAWBERRY ICED TEA

Since strawberries contain so much water, they easily dissolve in drinks.

1 cup strawberries, hulled and halved
2 tablespoons sugar
4 cups water
4 bags black tea, such as Lipton

Combine berries, sugar, and water in saucepan. Bring to boil. Remove from heat and add tea bags. Steep 5 minutes, then remove tea bags and cool. Strain mixture into pitcher. Serve over ice in tall glasses.

SERVES 4

"We are to walk about your gardens, and gather the strawberries ourselves, and sit under trees...and it is all to be out of doors...."
　　　　—*Jane Austen,* Emma

BERRY SANGRIA

Keep a pitcher full of fruity sangria in the fridge for unexpected summertime guests.

1 bottle Chianti *or* other fruity red wine
1 orange, halved and sliced
1 cup small strawberries, hulled and quartered
juice of 3 oranges

Pour the wine into a pitcher. Add orange slices and berries. Chill 3 hours. Pour in orange juice, stir well, and chill until serving time. Serve in iced glasses, spooning fruit into each serving.

MAKES 1 QUART

STRAWBERRY MARGARITAS

If you like your margaritas on the pink and fruity side, this is the one for you.

1 cup strawberries, hulled
¼ cup lime juice
¼ cup tequila
1 tablespoon orange liqueur, such as Cointreau *or* Grand Marnier
1½ cups crushed ice
2 whole strawberries, with stems
2 lime wedges

Combine berries, lime juice, tequila, and orange liqueur in blender. Add ice. Process until blended. Pour into two stemmed glasses and garnish each with a berry and a lime wedge.

SERVES 2

STRAWBERRY SHOTS

*To get that cocktail chatter going, surprise your
guests with these booze-injected berries. Zap—the
professional flavor injector—is an inexpensive gadget
available at well-stocked hardware and cookware
stores.*

tequila *or* vodka
liqueur, such as Cointreau, creme de strawberry,
    or cassis
large whole strawberries, with stems

In a bowl, mix 2 parts tequila or vodka to 1 part
liqueur. Draw into flavor injector, then insert
near stem end of each berry and slowly inject
until liquor begins to spill back out of berry—
large berries have about a 1-teaspoon capacity.
Serve on tray at room temperature.

CONVERSIONS

LIQUID
1 Tbsp = 15 ml
½ cup = 4 fl oz = 125 ml
1 cup = 8 fl oz = 250 ml

DRY
¼ cup = 4 Tbsp = 2 oz = 60 g
1 cup = ½ pound = 8 oz = 250 g

FLOUR
½ cup = 60 g
1 cup = 4 oz = 125 g

TEMPERATURE
400° F = 200° C = gas mark 6
375° F = 190° C = gas mark 5
350° F = 175° C = gas mark 4

MISCELLANEOUS
2 Tbsp butter = 1 oz = 30 g
1 inch = 2.5 cm
all-purpose flour = plain flour
baking soda = bicarbonate of soda
brown sugar = demerara sugar
heavy cream = double cream
sugar = caster sugar